DEDICATION

To my Parents for all their support, wi
couldn't and wouldn't be writing this now.

PRO-LOG

FOURWORD

"Thanks
for
buying
this"

INTRODUCTION

My name is Stevie Vegas and I am a punaholic. I drink up to 3 gallons of Punahol every day. Only kidding (but then that's why you are here hopefully!)

I'm actually a Professional Juggler who entertains through comedy, music, magic & teaching Circus Skills. I also like to curl up into a tight ball, which is why I am an "All-round entertainer!"

Back in May 2016, I decided to publish a joke every day on Twitter and this habit has evolved to me currently (March 2024) putting up over 50 jokes each month and having a back catalogue of 4500+ jokes of which this jokebook contains 500!

Since 2019, I have reached the finals of the UK Pun Championships on 3 occasions, getting the chance to battle it out in a boxing ring at Leicester Comedy Festival in front of sell-out crowds of over 1,000! This was always my favourite show of the year to attend as a punter - and now I was a part of it! This introduced me to many Comedians who have gone on to be great friends.

In March 2020, when the world went a bit quiet, some of the comedians who had taken part in this contest decided to put on a livestream weekly show (every Sunday at 7pm) and they called it "The UK Pun-Off". I soon managed to get on board and as well as producing and hosting many shows, I have won it 4 times. This is now very much a live event which tours round the comedy festivals in the UK, and during our full run at this year's Edinburgh Fringe (August 2024), I thought it might be good to have something tangible to sell after each show, hence this jokebook!

The jokes are all family-friendly (as that's my style of humour) and sorted into categories. There are extra sections to help provide variety and these contain material I have written when taking part in Punderdome, Punnit and also some Pun-Runs from my half-time entertainment slot on OutPUNched.

It's A Punder Fool Life:
500+ Jokes from an All-Round Entertainer

DEDICATION / PROLOGUE / FOREWORD
INTRODUCTION

Books
Celebrations
Clothing

A Pun Run on Clubs

Countries / Cities / Towns
Crime & Pun-ishment
Farming

PUNNIT: James Bond versus Cheese

Fitness / Exercise
Fruit

Punderdome: Personal Hygiene

Movies
Music

PUNNIT: Sport versus Sea Creatures

Pets
Social Media

A Pun Run on the Stock Market

Vegetables
Winter

THANKS

Books

Juggling with some overdue library books. One Librarian shouted "Outstanding", and the other said it was "Fine".

How did I find out that the ink in my pen had run out? I had a tip-off.

Feeling very optimistic about my attempt to steal every Charles Dickens book from my local library. In fact, I have great expectations.

I've been snowed under with requests to write a book about surviving avalanches.

In the Army, I guarded the first 5 Books of The Bible. It was my Torah duty.

I require one final sentence for my zombie book by tomorrow. That's my dead-line.

Thinking of adding pictures of flowers at the start of my next book. I think that's pretty foreword thinking.

My friend is way too keen to proofread my book about vampires. She's always asking for the necks chapter.

The entrance to the library car park has been made from crushed books. Now that's a novel approach!

Been reading all about a guy who kept meticulous notes about his unhealthy bowel movements back in the 1600's. It's Samuel Pepys Diaorrhoea.

The Beastie Boys have decided to publish our latest report without giving me credit. They are very welcome to Parts B and C, but "I'm gonna fight for the right to Part A"

A Top Scottish crime-writer has agreed to rate all my jokes tonight in order of funniness. It's "Ian, Rankin"

My knowledge of partially drawn comic books is a bit sketchy.

The incident where my brother told tales on me staying in bed and I retaliated by sending up a mini-copter to spy on him, is covered in my new book "The Lie-in, The Snitch, and the War-drone".

The book about my favourite underground room has become a best cellar.

Of all the kindly Children's Authors, it's only R.L Stine that gives me the Goosebumps.

Whenever I can't think up a new joke, I leave my house and turn right to walk down Shakespeare Street, Keats Way, Tennyson Drive and Wordsworth Avenue. It soon cures my writers block.

I keep pictures of all my fights in a scrapbook.

A Spiderman actor is now starring in a Shakespeare play. "Tobey or not Tobey, that is the question…"

Instead of reading reports, I skip to the end. I'm always jumping to conclusions.

The sisters who wrote Wuthering Heights and Jane Eyre wrote a musical where a group of guys stripped for charity. It was "The Full Bronte".

If you are looking for my book about punching wooden displays, it doesn't hit the shelves until tomorrow…

To help decide which comic book I would borrow, I put an Asterix next to my favourites.

I didn't win the story-writing contest, so I'm changing the rules so my friend is the sole judge. I've said to him, "I'll win next year… you mark my words".

Decided to write a book about what I was going to do during Lockdown. It's my Ought To Biography.

Bought two bookshelves. One was already made up, so I'll use the other one for my non-fiction.

Almost finished a new streetwise version of the Harry Potter books. I'll soon be Rowling innit?

My book on how to find the most conches on a beach has become a Best-Sheller.

Why was the Shepherd unable to use his oversized writing set? The sheep kept running out of the pen.

I was given a book about how to be grateful. Just wishing there was some way I could say thanks...

Did my annual stocktake. Found a couple of Dandy's and a Beano.

Almost finished writing my novel about a house with just one window left open. I'm on my final draft.

Wasn't able to write the definitive guide about the tribe that established Pre-Columbian America as I ran out of Inca.

To lose some weight, I've decided to only eat food that has never been mentioned in any recipe book since the invention of the printing press. It's a Gutenberg-free diet.

I used to run an A4 paper business, but it folded. Thankfully this meant I had an A5 booklet business instead.

Tried to grab my partner's romantic novels, but I was told to keep my hands to my shelf.

How did my friend know she might give birth to a pen? Let's just say she had a little inkling.

Shakespeare sometimes amended his poetry while running backwards, so he could quip to his onlookers that he was re-versing.

> I need to put one final bit of punctuation at the end of Mr. Twain's biography, any ideas?

> Question mark?

> I can't, he died in 1910.

Celebrations
(Parties/Weddings/Birthdays etc)

When fitting into your giant turkey outfit for a Christmas party, it's best if you hold an onion. Otherwise, it takes sages.

To celebrate Indiana Jones' birthday, we had a whip round.

Really enjoyed the Referee's retirement party. It was a great send-off.

> I assisted in the birth of Winnie the Pooh's friend, then we had some food to celebrate.

> Deliver Roo?

> No, I cooked.

When I told my fiancée that I had booked our honeymoon in outer space, she was over the moon!

To celebrate the fall of a French Military Fortress, I punched a fish. It was Bashed Eel day.

When I went to the Winter Olympics party, I brought Eddie the Eagle. The invite had said to bring a jumper.

When I suggested my friend dress as a ghost for the Halloween party, he went as white as a sheet.

At today's Birthday event, a present was unwrapped when the music stopped. We uncovered fusili, then spaghetti, then macaroni. It was Pasta Parcel.

Don't worry, I have another 16 jokes about celebrations. 4 better, 4 worse, 4 richer and 4 much, much poorer.

> Bought a chocolate fountain and threw a party.

> Fondue?

> Well, everyone seemed to have a good time.

To celebrate our new scarlet, ruby and strawberry range of Dulux paints, we painted the town red.

My Marvel themed party went wrong when I forgot to invite all but just a couple of people. It was a Loki affair.

At the Cannibal-themed party, I went straight to the finger buffet.

If you want a quote for a Cockney birthday party, I can do you a good jelly deal...

An Irish band have agreed to sing at my next Hogmanay Party, then officially open my box of chocolates, so that's a Corrs for Celebration.

I had an amazing career making Wedding bouquets, then I just threw it all away.

Looking for the most reasonably priced scary figure to host your Halloween party? Try Ghost Compere!

I only began processing my own photos on my 90th birthday. I was a late developer.

If I were to phone the people at CERN and offer to throw a quick celebration, would that make me a party call accelerator?

In the Grand Final of musical statues, I faced some stiff opposition.

I appreciate when all the family put receipts in with the presents they have bought for Christmas. It allows for many happy returns.

An old friend drove straight at the entrance to my garden during a party. He was a gate-crasher.

Fred Flintstone is off to celebrate Christmas at a party in the United Arab Emirates. It's an Abu Dhabi do!

I'm trying to sell some ancient lengthy advertisement boards before midnight on 31st December.

4 Old Long Signs?

It's not time to sing that yet...

Thinking of putting all of my profits into a thermal clothing business while just wearing my undergarments. Should I in vest?

After I wash my clothes, I put them in a machine that doesn't want any thanks and is more than happy to heat them up. It's my humble dryer.

Sign in Charity shop – "Only 3 Items of Clothing allowed in Changing Room". Had to strip down to my shorts and socks so I could try on a jumper.

To discover which smart outfits I might wear in the future, I invented a tie machine.

Got my musical underwear caught on a post and it catapulted me forwards. I was flying by the beat of my pants..

My hooded fleece keeps listening into conversations and then gossiping about them. It's becoming a nosey parka.

Went to the therapist as I kept getting annoyed when my clothes didn't fit into my wardrobe. She said I have hanger management issues.

Currently going through a phase where I try on clothes that are exactly my size. I guess I'll grow out of it eventually.

Thought I had bought trousers with 50% off. They were shorts.

Glad I married a shoemaker. She's a great tidy upper.

I'm scared of tight sweaters made from rabbit fur. I have angoraphobia.

Can't believe you told that joke about wearing bladed footwear in a paddy field! You were skating on thin rice...

My new shoes are so painful that when I walk, my tongue sticks out.

Tried to do some embroidery at the local Community Centre, but they have a No Smocking Policy.

My Driving Instructor told me to change gear, so I went home and put on a different groovy suit.

I really like the bits at the end of Doc Marten boots.

Steel toe caps?

No, I'm happy to pay for them.

A Pun-Run on Clubs
(Excerpt from OutPUNched Show)

OutPUNched was a livestreamed show that ran for 12 episodes from May 2021 to October 2022. All episodes are available in a playlist on the @UKPunOff YouTube Channel. It was created and hosted by Iain MacDonald (@ImacPun), and featured me as a competitor in the first couple of episodes, after which I switched to being the comedy sidekick who helped with the scoring and infringements (such as pointing out when participants repeated a pun). At half-time in the shows, I would perform a 3-5min routine, and there are 2 of these pun-runs for you to enjoy in this jokebook. Here's the first!

Here are some of the many Clubs and Societies I have been involved with over many years, along with their first rules:

Alphabet Club: Always mind your P's and Q's

Magic Club: Pull a rabbit out of a hat (and not a hat out of a rabbit!)

Wood Turners Club: Don't worry about the first rule, as nothing is set in stone.

Operatic Club: Please state your aria of expertise,

Thesaurus Club: Do not talk, natter, gossip, chinwag, rabbit on and on and on...

Coercion Club: To do exactly what I say, exactly when I tell you to do it...

Geology Club: No rules. Just rock up!

You can find me performing a version of this routine by doing a YouTube search on "OutPUNched pun run on clubs".

Countries, Cities & Towns

You want me to bake a dessert in the shape of a famous Italian landmark? Pisa cake!

I'm addicted to saying goodbye to French people. So without further adieu…

My TikTok story about trains in Wales has just went via Rhyl.

You might think I got tattoos of an African country because I'd been there on holiday but it was actually to impress a girl. I had Algeria motifs.

Norway is apparently the most expensive country in the world, so I can't afjord to live there.

My favourite Caribbean island is Cuba. Always Havana good time there.

I have a question about what Beijing used to be known as, but the answer is on the next page. No Peking please!

Can I make jokes about the Volcano erupting or are we still waiting for the dust to settle?

There is an Icelandic custom of burning any Ladies who cast spells, then spreading their ashes over your Garden if you want to have a bumper crop. It's in Rake a Witch.

Need help tracing my Ancient European Ancestors. Anyone got some large thin paper and a shovel?

I've set up a business extracting shale oil with the members of Status Quo. We're "Fracking All Over the World".

I choked on a dry biscuit while in Venezuela's largest City.

Caracas?

No, it was a hob-nob.

Went to the Czech Republic to sit a test on the effects of touching people lightly and causing them to laugh. It was a Prague tickle exam.

Last time I visited Antarctica, I needed to poo constantly. I was in Continent.

Vatican City seems like a Pope-ular destination. Might Rome around there, then book a rest in Romania.

I've made a concrete statue of the former President of New Zealand. Just waiting for it to Ardern.

Machines in Africa are threatening to rule the world. The Botswana takeover.

The Optician says I should be careful when taking aluminium to America, as you can lose an "i".

My friend entertains by pretending to be a Russian Prince. He's always Igor to please.

"Mr. Schwarzenegger doesn't seem to be welcome in certain parts of Ireland."

"Killarney?"

"No, they just don't like him."

I WRITE ALL MY JOKES IN CAPITALS. THIS ONE WAS WRITTEN IN EDINBURGH.

Just wondering if I could drive to France, and then try to hit you with a bow and arrow? I know it's a long shot...

Designed a provocative T-shirt based on famous cities in Italy. It has holes cut out in the chest area, so you can see both my Naples.

I'm studying "A Christmas Carol" at a German University. B.A Hamburg!

There's a great website for discovering the best places to visit in Libya. Tripoli-advisor!

> I got first prize in the Canadian Clothes Drying Championships.

> Win a Peg?

> No, but I got a lovely trophy.

When I visited the capital of South Africa, everyone was dressed as Batman or Superman. It was Cape Town.

My last job was as a cleaner for the Ruler of Saudi Arabia. I had to move the Sheikh, then Vac, then put the freshness back.

Teamed up with The Prodigy to compose a new theme tune for a Belgian detective. I'm the Poirot starter!

> I'm visiting the Netherlands to fetch a cereal crop from my favourite 80's group.

> Holland Oates?

> No, I can't go for that.

Had a sudden urge to pee as I flew north over Fiji, so I went Tuvalu.

Saw some Flamenco dancing in Spain, then felt unwell. I had Sevilla chest pains.

My French joke about bonbon sweets is just two good.

If you can't find any cigars in Cuba, your next port of call should be Trinidad and Tobacco.

If you want me to make a joke about Eastern Europe, then So-viet.

> Can anyone teach me how to say "But, Yes" in French?

> Mais oui?

> Oh, go on then.

An Australian has invented a potion that stops people being unable to think clearly. It's an Addle-Aide.

There are over 534 million people who speak Spanish, not just Juan.

Was looking for a motor sport to play in Senegal, so I got in Dakar… then found a rally.

"Next episode of South Park will be based in Ireland."

"Kilkenny?"

"Yeah, they do it every week."

Later on this evening, I shall be showing you an actual size map of Europe. Let's see how that unfolds.

Asked the New Zealand team to help me with some computer coding, as they are all expert Haka's.

"Took my Dog to an Irish County to get him shampoo'd."

"Antrim?"

"No, just a shampoo."

Crime & Pun-ishment

The gang tried to break into the Jam Jar Factory, but they just couldn't pull it off!

To stop the guy with a horn breaking into my house, I installed a bugler alarm.

I've got a number plate and 2 large heavy doors for sale. Don't tell anyone, but I got them off the back of a lorry.

I used to drive posh people around, then my car got nicked. Now I've got nothing to chauffer it.

Thieves broke into the cough sweet factory after security forgot to locket.

It was so hot in the Jury Room today, that we demanded "Just Ice".

Which Detective kept stumbling across the clues and solved the murder accidentally?
Sheer luck Holmes.

After I robbed the Bronzing Salon, I twisted my ankle, so I forced someone nearby to give me a piggyback. Sorry, I'm going off on a tanned gent...

I was a lazy Hitman. Always missed my deadlines.

Whoever committed this crime had visited previously and left behind some painkillers. I think it was pre-medicated...

First to arrive at the autopsy lab, gets to open the male.

Every time I kill someone, I write down all of their vital statistics. I am literally getting a weigh with murder.

As a Lawyer, I knew exactly what the Prisoner was about to say. They were kind enough to let me finish their sentences.

Went to H.M Prison. The King wasn't in.

I strangled the clown, then pushed the tightrope walker off the rope. It was my Circus Kills Workshop.

My favourite gangster was the one who would lift his enemies by their underwear. Wedgie Kray.

When my friends and I stole the car, one took the wheels, another grabbed the engine. As they arrived first, I had to take a back seat on this one.

They found me with my phone plugged in using the cable I had stolen. Guilty as charged.

I looked after my gang for our gold heists and made sure there was no bullion going on.

> Julia Roberts and I robbed a Flower Shop.

> Steal magnolias?

> No, we went straight for the till.

Whoever succeeded in opening up all my luggage, you have got away with it. The case is now closed.

When my Manager interrupted a conversation to ask me if I could sleep in the office tonight to prevent any burglaries, I told him to mind his own business.

I admit to vandalising the picture made up of terracotta tiles. It's time for me to face the mosaic...

Been mugged by a crab who has taken my last bit of money, and now I'm starting to feel the pinch…

Currently developing a sitcom about a murder in an airport. Just about to shoot the pilot.

The thieves managed to avoid capture until they ran into a 60's dance contest. I caught my nickers in the twist.

Want to buy next weeks exam paper? No questions asked…

Just wait till I find the guy who stole my spinal support. Hold me back!

Before sentencing, the judge had some food with an Association of Craftspeople. He then announced "Guild Tea as charged".

The football officials kindly stopped the match after 90mins so that I could take part in a murder trial. It was in jury time.

Spotted the police heading into the National Portrait Gallery. I wonder if they are going to frame somebody?

Farming

I gave up on my wind farm after the cows got caught on the propellors.

I get a bad headache when people steal the crops from my field. It's My grain!

Saw a bloke wandering around the countryside shouting "Loadsamoney". It was Harry in field.

I got told I was rubbish at being a Shepherd, but I won't lose any sheep over it.

Using semaphore, I have invented a new way to tell Farmers that their favourite stabled animal has sadly passed away. I've put a lot of time into it, so I hope I'm not flagging a dead horse.

My farm was so small, that all the cows could produce was condensed milk.

Got a job deterring young delinquents from stealing cereal crops. I am quite literally trying to separate the wheat from the Chav's.

Been awarded "Pig Pen Perfumer of the Year". Judges were impressed with my de-stinked style.

I usually buy Chinese cooking equipment on the way home from a countryside ramble. I love going for a wok.

Anyone need one thousand bales of hay? I've got stacks!

To keep track of the daily going-on's at the farm, I wrote about it in my dairy.

When I pushed over the farmer and stole his churn and some milk, I was arrested for assault and buttery.

I don't care what the grains in a field have to say about any topic. I'm wheat intolerant.

When I took the farmers on every ride at the fairground, we had a field day!

To remember how many trees I've cut down, I keep a log.

When my cow passed away, I followed him into the Underworld so I could turn his hide into a purse. I went hell for leather.

In my spare time, I like to coax cows into large paper bags and take them home. I'm a cattle rustler.

To increase the yield of all the rice in the field, try adding some pasta-cides.

PUNNIT:
James Bond Versus Cheese!

Punnit is a podcast that I have appeared on twice. This episode was recorded in November 2020. I was competing against World Slam-Poetry champion Harry Baker, and I did reasonably well! The idea of this show is that contestants are given (in advance) 2 topics that they have to mash together to create puns. They each get to tell 5 of these puns, then the host of the show picks a winner for that round.

1. Diamonds are for Cheddar   (it goes well with some Shirley BASS-ey).
2. George Lazenbrie
3. Man with the Gorgon Gun   or   Gorgon-Eye
4. Cathedral Royale
5. Holly Goudahead from The Spy Who Loved Halloumi
6. Die Another Dairylea
7. Goudafinger
8. Tomozzarella Never Dies
9. Fromage Roquefort with Love
10. Timothy Stilton
11. Roger Leerdammoore
12. The Wedge Is Not Enough
13. Sean Caerphilly
14. Monteraker or Moon Roquefort
15. Swissy Galore
16. No Time to Die(t)
17. Little Smellie (You Only Live Twice) - Little Nellie was a bright yellow autogyro plane

Punnit Podcast should be available from wherever you listen to your podcasts. This episode hasn't yet been released, but hopefully it will be one day!

Fitness / Exercise

My footwear isn't strong enough, so I'm sending them to Boot Camp.

I keep my brain in a jar, but keep forgetting to take it with me when I exercise. Can anyone help jog my memory?

Because I am much lazier than I used to be, I am getting a trophy... No wait, it's atrophy...

While wearing my pedometer and twerking, I discovered I had walked 15 Miley's.

I'm working as an Exercise Mat today. Well it's something to fall back on, innit?

Planning to run a Marathon in 6 months. That's only 0.145 miles per day, so should be achievable.

I performed for an elite group of hurdlers. Venue was packed to the Gunnall's.

They've got a new machine at the gym. It's very expensive and I can only use it for about an hour before I start to feel sick. It's called the "Vending Machine".

I think my laptop might be haunted. Might have to switch it off and go do some exorcising instead.

I have opened an eating establishment for Mo Farrah, Usain Bolt and all their athlete friends. It's a fast dude restaurant.

To get a six-pack, I've been advised to go down a hill in an inflatable ball. It's can be quite ab-zorbing!

Norman Cook is refusing to exercise and keeps eating snacks. He plans on changing his name to Slim Boy Fat.

I intended to go for a long walk today to get some exercise but I put my shoes on the wrong feet. If you see anyone wandering around in size 13 Nike's, can you ask them to return my shoes please?

When the gym instructor said he had added more weights to my exercise equipment, I thought he was pulling my leg.

Exercising with the army is the best way to keep up your Corps strength.

I found a local newspaper editor lying unconscious and phoned 999. They asked me to check his circulation, so I did some digging around and was able to report that he'd sold 9 copies this week.

BBC to make 1,000 episodes about ultra-distance marathons. They hope it will be a long-running drama.

I play Scrabble at my local gym and the prize is always protein powder to help build up my muscles. I've certainly got a whey with words.

Mr. Branson has offered me £1m if I can train him to run the Marathon in under 2hrs. I think it's just a get Rich quick scheme.

Found some rope in a large bin outside a builder's yard. Going to set up a skip higher business.

New feature on my Fitbit. If I fall over while exercising, it bounces me off the ground. It promises I will be up and running again in no time.

Called my trainer to find out how my 6-pack is developing. He wasn't picking up, so I left a message on his abswerphone.

I was bodybuilding outside and my dumbbells got wet, so I decided to put them on the clothes dryer which instantly broke. I soon realised the airer of my weights.

I decided to run a Marathon. Now I've got to find a venue, hire a team and do lots of paperwork.

Fruit

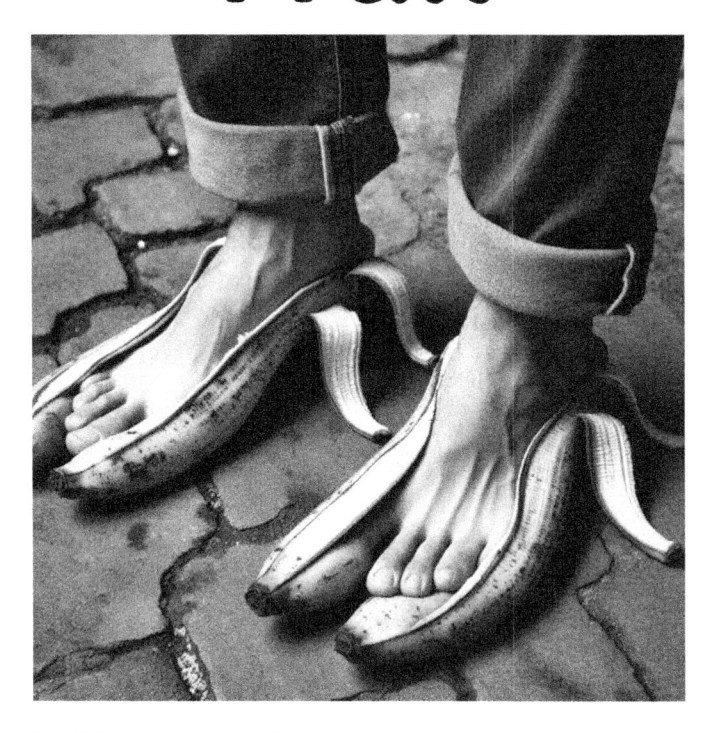

*Tired of having to throw your banana skins out?
Why not make them into a pair of slippers?*

Not sure I can have just one favourite fruit. Would anyone mind if I picked a pear?

My convict friend has been placing banana skins near all the exits to the prison. He is hoping to get out on a peel.

Really wanted to purchase a Hot Cross Bun for all my jokebook readers today but I didn't have enough in my currant account.

Ordered too many citrus fruits. I'll need to eat them by the zest-before date!

Took ages to be served in the Fruit and Nut shop, as one of the Cashew's is off sick.

Trying to win lots of fruit on Ebay. My currant bid is 50p.

I usually walk to Waitrose to buy all my posh fruit, but I 'av a car, d'oh!

When I stole citrus fruit from the gangster, I was living on borrowed lime...

I fell in love with someone who trod on grapes to make wine. Well it was more of a crush really...

When sculpting frozen fruit, it is important to view the result through a fresh pear of ice.

When I reported that thieves have broken in and stole all my fruity drinks, the police told me this is part of an Um-Bongoing Investigation.

I don't know much about pears, so I went to a Conference.

If you want to remember to eat certain sweet fruits, should you put a date in your diary?

A girl group gave me a hard plastic case for my fruit. It was banana armour.

Apple pastry factories without adequate barriers to prevent their workers falling in are likely to experience a large turnover of Staff.

To get the fruit machine working, I had to add an electrical currant.

Wrote a joke about electrocuting an apple. It will shock you to the core.

Writing a poem about dried fruit, that is picked during the summer season. Not sure why I began this task. There isn't much rhyme or raisin...

Punderdome Quarter-Final

Punderdome is a New York based show that I was asked to appear on during their 10th Anniversary (episode #123) on 6 May 2021 via webcam. It was 12.45am in the UK when they were doing the livestream, so I needed to have my wits about me! Contestants are given a topic and have just 2 minutes to prepare a 2-minute routine which they instantly perform, featuring as many puns as possible. The audience then voted, and I was put through to the semi-final. Big thanks to Fred Firestone & the Punderdome Community for their friendship & encouragement.

I'll start with toothbrushes; well I'll give it a twirl *[I twirled some toothbrushes on a stick]!* It's a very full filling thing to do and will have you bristling with confidence. But that's interdental...

My computer keeps spraying me with deodorant every time I type a password. It's a Brut force attack. I'm Sure you have that brand in America, if not Mum's the word... and in the Church of the Deodorant, let us spray...

So I hope to make a Clean getaway with all these. I used to be a helpful Plumber, so I'll just let that sink in... and I used to keep razors in my shoe. Always got to places in the nick of time.

I used to use wash and go, but *[zig-zag card trick where the middle of the card disappears],* but mine didn't have any extra body in it...

This is called a 3-ball shower *[I demonstrated a triangular juggling pattern]*, and I usually do it with babies, so it would be a baby shower... I'm getting a bit washed up now. I like the smell of lavender as I talk to people. It's a common scents approach...

You can find me performing this routine by doing a YouTube search on "Punderdome 10th Anniversary highlights".

Movies

I keep on buying Groundhog Day, then arriving home to discover I already own it!

It's easy to make tea for the Hobbits. You just put one Baggin'.

Due to the rising cost in fuel, the next Fast and Furious film won't have any Diesel.

I've written the script for a low budget film starring Harrison Ford and a tiny piece of jewellery. It'll be made by an Indy Pendant Company.

I enjoy spraying the supporting characters of Disney's "Lion King" onto buildings. I'm a Rafiki artist.

My house is cleaner since I got rid of 101 Dalmations. In fact it's spotless!

I'm in charge of trying to get Jaws chosen as the number 1 movie of all-time, but "we're gonna need a bigger vote".

The headmaster at Hogwarts liked to make a big entrance. It was Professor Double Door.

Written a screenplay where you see Bruce Willis filling in a form once every 10 years since the early 1970's. It's called "The Sixth Census".

On the "Muppets in Space" sequel, we get to witness the first Mahna Mahna on the Moon.

The guy in my nightmares keeps dropping toasted crumbs for me to follow. It was Bready Krueger.

There's a remake of the 2nd Star Trek film which features Captain Kirk's elderly relative having a nice soak. "Star Trek 2: The Bath of Gran".

Hugh Jackman insists on being called Wolverine on every film he is in. He put the claws in his contract.

Captain America lined up and rolled his glass bead, knocking several out the ring, then Thor angrily smashed them with a hammer. That's the latest goings on in the Marble Universe.

For the remake of Flash Gordon, I hear that Brian Blessed is in with a good shout.

Remember the time that Disney hired me to increase the optical colours in all the woodland creatures on their Bambi film? Well that was my bright-eyed deer.

Managed to swallow the entire DVD Boxset of James Bond, then I got the Living Daylights kicked out of me.

When I read the book about villains in the Peter Pan movie and how they got their comeuppance, I was hooked from the beginning. That's Smee finished now.

Whoopi Goldberg used my bathroom and broke the water tank, so that's the Cistern knacked.

When I last visited the seaside, an action hero swooped down and stole my chips. It was Steven Seagull.

Have you ever noticed that Darth Vader looks like all the other Darth baddies? I guess when you've seen one, you've seen a Maul.

Wrote a film about a Mum who gives birth to a boy who immediately speaks in a posh accent. "Look Who's Tarquin".

You can go from Disneyworld straight to the Harry Potter Studio Tour, if you go through the Dumbo-door…

The Singer of that Fame song helped me with some DIY, then Jim Carrey popped round to show me one of his movies from the 90's. It was Me, My Shelf and Irene.

I was summoned into the jungle to give the Predator a nice hairstyle. I was dreading it at first, but he's a really nice guy!

Filming a movie where Mr. Grant designs an illegible typeface to spell out his first name, and adds a figure on the end of it. "4 Wingdings and a Numeral"

Submitted my script for a film about traffic signals. Hoping to get the green light.

The Barbie sequel will be this Christmas. For the main song, I've arranged to walk Ken in a Winter Wonderland.

Finding out which movie company made Top Gun Maverick is of Paramount importance.

> Bruce Willis is to team up with Milla Jovovich, and ride across the Alps in a tribute to Hannibal, but he insisted he didn't want to ride near the front or the back of the expedition.

> The Fifth Elephant?

> That'll do nicely!

Speaking of Tom Hanks earlier films, I'm a Big fan.

When E.T let me ride his bike, I was over the moon!

Dumbo has just written his Autobiography. It's called Memoir-y of an Elephant.

Jules Verne crashed his shipping container and the vegetables went overboard. This was the inspiration for 20,000 leeks under the sea.

> People keep taking me to coffee shops and then telling me how rubbish my gangster impressions are.

> Crap Pacino?

> Ooh yes please, with 2 sugars...

Julie Andrews kept clearing her throat on the film set. It was the sound of mucus.

> My favourite actor from Guardians of the Galaxy enjoys making rodent flavour snacks.

> Crisp Rat?

> Yeah, that's the fella!

Will Smith has been appointed head of Security at a Videoconferencing firm. Their new slogan is "Yo Backup now, and give a Brother Zoom".

> My former wife kept meticulous records of all the sci-fi films we watched.

> Ex files?

> and Star Wars, Bladerunner...

Where can you find your lost Little Mermaid figures? Under the seat!

Keanu refuses to do any Magic throughout the year except for one month, when he'll bend over backwards at the chance to perform. It's the May Tricks.

Am I worried that I won't do well in the movie action heroes nicknames exam? Not in the Sly test.

Been in France to investigate who the bell ringer in the Disney movie was. My last hunch? Back in Notre-Dame.

> Wondering which Bruce Lee film I should submit to a contest.

> Enter the Dragon?

> Yeah, I could do, but I think Fist of Fury was better

My DVD has an advert featuring a man holding on to a giant "P" & "G" while moving around to music. I think it's to encourage Pay Rental Guy Dance.

The film "Hunt for Red October" was based on a crew story.

Is Angry Birds The Movie a Chick-Flick?

> Clint Eastwood got his first big break after a talent scout spotted him being dragged by a horse with his foot caught in the stirrups.

> Rawhide?

> Yeah, huge hole in the back of his trousers too...

Asked my drunk friend who his favourite actress was, but the response came out all Garbo'd.

Music

Had to ban the cats from setting up their own DJ business. They kept scratching my records.

When you join Fleetwood Mac's darts team, you can throw your own way…

I took Agnetha, Benny, Bjorn and Anni-Frid down the side of a Mountain. We went ABBA-seiling.

"When the band began singing "Don't Dream It's Over", I felt claustrophobic.

Crowded House?

No, it was a really packed Concert Hall."

If you want to remove some 80's pop lyrics from a sheet of paper, can you use an Erasure?

Found KSI, Skepta and Dizzee Rascal chucking away all their songs from my CD collection. They were clearing the Garage out.

> Wondering what song I should ask Diana Ross to sing?

> Upside Down?

> Ok, I am wondering what song I should ask Diana Ross to sing

Frank Sinatra kept all the songs he wanted to sing on a To Do Be Do List.

My stomach gets upset and criticises me every time I perform in a talent contest. I must be suffering from Irritable Cowell Syndrome.

"I don't regret saving my work in a Portable Document Format." Edith PDF

Kylie's been living at the bottom of my garden for a few months now. I just can't get her out of my shed.

I want to visit the Spanish Steps. I've been there at least Cinco, Seis, Siete, Ocho times.

Was given the choice between singing "The Logical Song" during lunch or helping the homeless. It was soup or tramp.

I was in court yesterday having been accused of hitting The Blockheads with their rhythm stick. Took ages, as we had to wait on the Dury to return. They found me not guilty, so that's a Reason to be Cheerful!

Fat 70's Scottish Band. "Obesity Rollers".

I couldn't have committed the crime as I was waving farewell to the lead singer of UB40. I have the perfect Ali-bye.

Refused to sign up to a heavy metal band's mailing list, as I didn't want to receive any Anthrax in the post.

Can't help thinking that the group "Boston" are in danger. It's more than a feeling…

When I sang "Groove is in the Heart" at karaoke, the audience were Deee-lite'd!

Had a dream that John Lennon was selling views at a nudist beach from behind a wooden fence. Imagine all the peepholes!

Been asked to tour with The Beautiful South but I told them "I need a little time, to think it over".

Inspiration for Dame Vera Lynn's most famous song came from when she was repeatedly fed blubber. "Whale Meat Again".

I wanted to remix the sound my heater makes and release it as a single, but it has a note on the front that says "Do not cover".

Trying to learn the Doh Ray Mi song. Soh Fah so good...

Thought of a joke about Frankie Goes to Hollywood, so I can relax now. Although several friends have said "Don't do it".

After I sang "All Rise" and "One Love", two of the band turned up, out of the Blue...

Next Friday on BBC4 "Bill Withers in Concert". Poor guy. Surely they could have kept him hydrated and in the shade, as they knew it was gonna be a lovely day...

Ms Minaj's leg is bleeding heavily, what should I do?

Tourniquet?

Not sure she should go on stage right now...

It's impossible to kill Celine Dion by cutting her up into tiny pieces. Her Heart Will Go On.

The Bee Gee's have gone back to work as ambassadors for an intergovernmental organisation that helps to promote peace and security. U.N Again.

The sweetest 80's singer? Simon Le Bon-Bon.

Imagining the newspaper headline if the E-Street Band ever helped a youth escape from jail. "Bruce Springs Teen".

Playing hide & seek with Hank Marvin. Can't seem to find him as he is lurking about in the shadows.

Props for "Removal Men - The Musical" can be picked up from the Box Office.

I was drowning when the lead singer of Destiny's Child happened to float by. Very thankful for my Beyonce Aid.

> Stuck in a long queue behind the band that sung "Why does it always rain on me", as they have ordered a load of hot drinks.

> It's a Travis tea.

> I wouldn't go that far, but it is annoying.

I was instrumental in getting rid of all the singers in my band.

I heard about Mike and the Mechanics through word of mouth.

I have taken to singing "Kayleigh" and "Lavender" like a Fish out of Marillion.

If you paint a portrait of Amy Winehouse crying, the tears dry on their own.

What do you get when you cross a pop star with some shades? Sunny and Cher.

I put a gravestone beside where Sandy Shaw perished in the quicksand, so there is always something there to remind me…

Tried to collaborate with Justin Timberlake on a new song over Zoom, but we couldn't get our connections in-sync.

> Bought a stability aid that previously used by a German Composer.

> Hans Zimmer?

> No, it was Beethoven's crutches.

Which member of Guns N Roses keeps all his tour dates in a Microsoft document? Excel Rows!

Which Boney M song has the most streams? Rivers of Babylon.

Game Show idea. Eat individually wrapped chocolates with Heather from M People, take an X-Ray and search for the Heroes inside yourself.

I'm Ampidextrous. I can listen to 2 songs at the same time.

If I say "Nutbush City Limits" and "Simply the Best", don't worry, it's just a Turner phrase…

An 80s band are buying drinks if you can authentically cry in front of them. It's Tears for Beers.

Tried to lift up one of The Hollies. He ain't heavy, but he did wriggle around a bit.

I was playing Twister with Abba earlier, but they kept annoying me by asking "What's the Name of the Game?"

> What do you think of the way I have reorganised my collection of KC & The Sunshine Band memorabilia?

> That's the way I like it!

Taylor Swift has just asked me to recommend a tour of South-West England. I said I wouldn't in Dorset.

A song about oversized clothing was at number forty and rose to number one in just one week. It was a big jumper.

After I ran over all of Musical Youth, I passed them crutches on the left hand side.

Which boy band were knocked off a Cliff by a South-Westerly gale? Wind Direction.

When I heard that someone had purchased me some expensive airbuds, it was music to my ears!

If I had to choose my favourite teenage pop magazine, then Smash Hits doesn't get a Look-in.

Currently formatting my biography of Bros and working out the final chapter. Should I use a Matt or Goss finish?

Got a job holding a long musical note, but I just couldn't sustain it.

Got a musical money forging kit. It makes banknotes.

When I pick up my phone, it emits the sounds of Mr. Manilow singing with a voice between tenor and bass. I think it's a Barry tone.

Listen out for me in a musical all about cake ingredients. I sing "sugar".

If you tap dance barefoot, is this sole music?

If you would like to dance, but are unable to kick your legs above your head, then join me in performing the Can't Can't.

Before I kill my victims, I sing them a top 40 song. I'm a hitman.

Do you know what really put my teeth on Edge? When I devoured 1/4 of U2.

I asked Gloria Gaynor if she would put sugar into ten cups of tea, but she replied "I will stir 5".

I had an energy drink, then my IPod instantly downloaded "Mull of Kintyre". I guess Red Bull really does give you Wings.

PUNNIT:
Sports Versus Sea Creatures!

This podcast was recorded in November 2020. My other entry can be found earlier in the jokebook along with an explanation of the show.

1. Golphin
2. Shrimpronysed Swimming
3. Otter Polo
4. Moby Dickathlon / Duckathlon
5. 110m Hurd-Eels
6. Cod-Sleighing
7. Beluge-a Whale
8. Godzillacrosse
9. Clay Penguin Shooting
10. Crabaddi
11. TiddlyWinkles
12. SpongeBobSleigh Squashpants
13. MMA - Mixed Mackerel Arts
14. Mantathon
15. Squid Skating
16. Pelicanoe Slalom
17. Jaws-Jitsu
18. Jousting-ray
19. Basquidball

Punnit Podcast should be available from wherever you listen to your podcasts. This episode hasn't yet been released.

Pets

*I gave my Hamster a strong coffee.
Can't have him falling asleep at the wheel.*

My cats enjoy drinking hot beverages then coughing it up again. It's hairball tea.

I couldn't get in my parrot's vehicle as I'd lost macaw keys.

Really chuffed with the Dogs I trained as pilots. They passed with flying collars!

I asked my pet snakes to help me build a wooden structure in the garden. Apparently, they are good at shedding.

I have bought an automatic cat feeder. Now I need to buy some automatic cats.

To find out how effective the rodent trap is on my new website, you hover the mouse over it.

I wasn't just a bit scared that someone would cook my dog for a second time, I was pet re-fried.

My attempt to teach rats how to fly was only partially successful. Oh well... you wing some, you lose some.

Easiest way to identify a Lizard is to see if they weigh their food before eating it. They have scales.

My Dog is an expert in sniffing out where I hide my liquorice sweets. He's a Bassett Hound.

I'm not usually a fan of animals, but that Russian Dog that was the first into Space? I really Laika.

I've employed Boy George as an animal whisperer. He's currently trying to calm a chameleon.

While my dog was being kept in overnight at the vet's, they offered a courtesy cat.

Do you think I've heard anything from my Puppy since the meat disappeared from the Kitchen counter? Not a sausage!

After my cat kept throwing up lots of hair on top of my favourite clothing, I had to issue my first furball warning.

> Thinking of making a TV show about training canines to cope with everything life throws at them.

> Dog you mentor, eh?

> Probably more of a reality show to be honest.

Went with Paula Abdul to find her a new puppy. She looked at a few, then went back to the first one. It was 3 pets forward, 2 pets back.

Do I think Schroedinger put cats inside all these sealed containers? In some cases yes...

The phone rang, and it was a dog whose name I didn't recognise. I have collar ID on my phone.

About to launch my new dog walking business. No strong leads yet, but a visit to the pet shop should sort that out.

Really enjoyed the pantomime about a cat who isn't feeling well and goes to her local chemist shop to buy some medicine. "Puss in Boots."

Welcome to the Church of the Dogs. If you need a seat, I kennel pew.

> Saving up to pay for an operation as my cat ate a lot of loose change.

> How much money is in the kitty?

> Not sure until we get an X-Ray done.

My new reptile business requires some extra finance. Anyone want to be a snakeholder?

Social Media

I wrote an article about keeping a bee inside my motorcycle helmet. It's creating quite a buzz!

I've managed to find all my favourite Bands and Artists on Social Media.

Tik-Tokking Heads

HashTest Dummies

LinkedIn Park

Snapchatta Khan

Reddit Chili Peppers

Justin Bebo

MySpace Cyrus

and Tweetloaf
(he would do any Bing for love).

Now I know my main audience on Twitter are people who would like Botox, I'm hoping to uncrease my followers.

Visited a beginners sewing forum to ask "which machine is best". They told me to start a new thread. Wasn't sure what they meant, but I cottoned on eventually.

My computer keeps spraying me with men's deodorant every time I try to update my Facebook profile. I think it's a Brut force attack. Unable to click on any Lynx also.

The bugling forum I have been a part of for many years has closed down. I guess this is the last post.

If you are searching for my excellent birdwatching puns on Twitter, then you are in for a real tweet.

Currently parcelling people up and sending them around the world. If you want to join in, I can keep you posted?

Almost got a parking fine at the Latin Social Media awards, until someone reminded me to act quickly by sending a Car Pay D.M.

Set up a new website rating the best fish suppers I have ever eaten. It's called ChipAdvisor.

It's a difficult job to make sure that all my social media jokes are LinkedIn some way.

Someone keeps stealing my boots and placing them at the bottom of a chute. I've been on social media to complain, but people keep sliding into my DM's.

I blocked my toilet earlier. Can't have it saying such nasty things about me on social media.

If I were to send you video clips of every meal I have ever eaten, would you subscribe to this feed?

I am going to win the "Best Post on Twitter" award by any memes necessary!

A Pun-Run on the Stock Market
(Excerpt from OutPUNched Show)

Hi I'm Stevie Vegas, and this is the latest financial news. Let's start with some good news.
- Voices on helium are going up.
- Sales of mountains have reached their peak.
- Sales of spreadsheet software continue to Excel. A spokesman is quoted as saying "You have my Word for that".

There is some stability in the market for:
- Nappies which remain unchanged.
- Sales of pencil and sharpeners remain stationery.

And now some bad news:
- Balloons seem to be suffering the most. This could be due to inflation.
- Gardening branches that have remained closed during lockdown may have to cut some of their branches.
- Sales of faulty chainsaws may cost you an arm and a leg.
- Sales of irons are de-creasing.

News just in...
- Sales of smoothies have been re-juiced.
- Duck feathers in bedding are down.
- Analysts report that there is something fishy going on with sushi and customers may get a raw deal.

And sadly, I must report that:
- Sales of musical chords have diminished. This is mainly due to staff shortages, as they have all decided to go back to their roots.
- Mining equipment has hit rock bottom.
- The Glue Factory is now in solvent. It's certainly a sticky situation for everyone and certainly doesn't look Pritti.
- Deep-Sea Diving equipment has sunk to a new low. Workers seem to be under a lot of pressure.

You can find me performing a version of this routine by doing a YouTube search on "OutPUNched pun run on stock exchange".

Vegetables

Doctor told me that I'm not eating properly. I have therefore decided to remove the cucumber from my ear, and the carrot from up my nose.

Am I worried about mentioning vegetables in my jokes? Not nessa celery.

After my performance for a group of vegetables, the lettuces were kind enough to pay my taxi fare home. And that's just the tip off the iceberg.

Currently seeing little orange vegetables floating inside my eyeballs. Think I might be suffering from carroteracts.

My vegetable flavour crisps taste a bit fishy, so I e-mailed everyone to warn them, with the subject "Scam pea fries".

Becoming a Vegetarian was definitely a missed steak.

I am the polite person in charge of frozen vegetables and managing the long lines of customers at Iceland. Always minding my peas and queues.

My story about out-of-date vegetables has been leeked. The press are about to turnip at my door.

My bus helps pull up vegetables. It's a root master.

Been eating lots of carrots recently as my boss says I need super vision.

I knew we needed to buy more vegetables when someone rearranged the lettuce on the fridge door.

Winter

"I took a selfie with an elusive Snowman."

"Abominable?"

"No, it turned out OK."

Car was frozen over with sugary cereals, so I de-frostied it.

A family member lent me a vehicle to get down the snowy hill to a concert. It was Sister's Sledge.

I've invested in a little heater to warm them up before they ring the doorbell. No more cold callers!

At the snow-clearing championships in Scandinavia, I was steam captain.

Revamping a musical about a circus that tours only during the winter months. "The Greatest Snowman".

Apparently there's 12 inches of snow in Dallas. I don't remember that episode though…

Fastest long-distance runner during the Winter months is Snow Farrah.

Due to the lack of winter venues to practice skiing nearby, I bought a load of muesli and poured it down a hill. I'll soon get used to Alpen skiing.

I thought I saw David Jason hanging around outside my window earlier. It turned out to be a Touch of Frost.

Looking for some coal to put on a snowman, and I fell down an open pit. Had to visit the Miner Injuries Unit.

Not going to have enough time to insulate all my pipes before the next cold snap. I'm lagging behind.

At the Cruft's Winter Special, my dog won "Best in Snow".

The extreme cold at the Winter Olympics made my toes curl.

I really love my de-icer. We get into a lot of scrapes.

The gritters are doing a great job. I hope they take this compliment with more than a pinch of salt.

Found a 3 of Hearts buried in the snow, then the 3 of Spades against my icy windscreen. I'm predicting a cold snap.

THANKS

To the #LunchPun, OutPUNched, UK Pun Off, Punderdome, UK Pun Championships and Punnit communities for all their encouragement, advice and good-natured competitiveness (which always brings out the best in a true joke-writer).

To all the punners who offered advice in writing my jokebook (might as well learn from the mistakes and triumphs of my fellow entertainers!) These included:

Paul Eggleston   (@pauleggleston)
Richard Pulsford   (@RichardPulsford)
Scott Montgomery (@ScottMo68256087)
Max Harvey   (@MaxHarvey79) (who also proof-read the book)

Also grateful to Chris "Alf" Leworthy (@WhoElseButAlf) who designed the awesome cover to this book.

All of the above-named people have jokebooks available on Amazon, which I highly recommend!

Special thanks to Iain MacDonald (@ImacPun) for his help and advice throughout the whole process and for prof-reeding with his very critical (but always constructive) feedback. He was very keen on capital punishment (I was capitalising too many words) so you can thank him that the jokes are much easier to read now!

Please give me a follow as an author on Amazon as well as the methods provided below:

For more information, please e-mail
steve@jugglingworld.biz

Be the first to see my new jokes by following on
Twitter / X: **@SteveJuggler**
(around 50 jokes each month)

Learn how to Juggle and how to book me to entertain at your events by visiting my website:

https://www.jugglingworld.biz

Copyright © 2024 Steve Thomson

The rights of Stevie Vegas to be identified as the author of this work has been asserted to him in accordance with the Copyright, Designs and Patents Act of 1988.

Main Joke Category Pictures created using AI.

I wonder if anyone actually reads this bit.

All rights reserved. No part of this book may be reproduced or used in any manner without written permission of the copyright owner except for the use of quotations in a book review.

First printed edition April 2024

Printed in Great Britain
by Amazon